# A Friend Is Someone Special

compiled by
Frederick Drimmer

Illustrations by
Julie Shearer Maddalene

The C.R. Gibson Company
Publishers
Norwalk, Connecticut

# A Friend Is
# Someone Special

Friendship is the feeling you possess for a particular person as distinct from all other persons. It is a very beautiful and intimate and close relationship which is destroyed if it is bestowed casually. To be able to say that you have a friend is to know that there is one person to whom your affairs are as important as his own, on whose aid and counsel and affection you can count in all times of trouble and distress, to whose aid you will fly the moment you hear he needs your help.

It is impossible for any man or woman to feel like that for more than a few persons.

ST. JOHN ERVINE

A friend is one who incessantly pays us the compliment of expecting from us all the virtues, and who can appreciate them in us.

The friend asks no return but that his friend will religiously accept and wear and not disgrace his apotheosis of him. They cherish each other's hopes. They are kind to each other's dreams.

HENRY DAVID THOREAU

A friend is a present you give yourself.

ROBERT LOUIS STEVENSON

This is my friend — through good or ill report
My friend. He who injures him by word or
    deed,
Were it but the thin film of an idle breath
Clouding the clear glass of a stainless soul,
He injures me.

RICHARD HOVEY

My best friend is the man who in wishing me
well wishes it for my sake.

ARISTOTLE

Don't walk in front of me —
    I may not follow.
Don't walk behind me —
    I may not lead.
Walk beside me —
    and just be my friend.

ALBERT CAMUS

If a man should importune me to give a
reason why I loved him, I find it could no
otherwise be expressed than by making an-
swer: because it was he, because it was I.

MICHEL DE MONTAIGNE

Depth of friendship does not depend upon length of acquaintance.

RABINDRANATH TAGORE

A mere friend will agree with you, but a real friend will argue.

RUSSIAN PROVERB

Love is flowerlike;
Friendship is a sheltering tree.
SAMUEL TAYLOR COLERIDGE

When there is a temper of sympathy in us it hardly matters whether we say little or much to others in company; the friendly smile, the ready attention, the kind pressure of a hand, is enough to make us understood by them, and to make all things known to us.

BENJAMIN JOWETT

Friendship is a strong and habitual inclination in two persons to promote the good and happiness of one another.

EUSTACE BUDGELL

Friendship is like two clocks keeping time.

UNKNOWN

All men have their frailties; and whoever looks for a friend without imperfections will never find what he seeks. We love ourselves notwithstanding our faults, and we ought to love our friends in like manner.

CYRUS

Know this, that he that is a friend to himself is a friend to all men.

SENECA

A faithful friend is an image of God.

FRENCH PROVERB

The test of friendship is assistance in adversity, and that, too, unconditional assistance. Cooperation which needs consideration is a commercial contract and not friendship. Conditional cooperation is like adulterated cement, which does not bind.

MAHATMA GANDHI

We are most of us very lonely in this world; you who have any who love you, cling to them and thank God.

WILLIAM MAKEPEACE THACKERAY

True friendship ought never to conceal what it thinks.

ST. JEROME

## I SAW IN LOUISIANA A LIVE-OAK GROWING

I saw in Louisiana a live-oak growing,
All alone stood it and the moss hung
    down from the branches,
Without any companion it grew there
    uttering joyous leaves of dark green,
And its look, rude, unbending, lusty, made
    me think of myself,
But I wonder'd how it could utter joyous
    leaves standing alone there without
    its friends near, for I knew I could not,
And I broke off a twig with a certain
    number of leaves upon it, and twined
    around it a little moss,
And brought it away, and I have placed it
    in sight in my room.

It is not needed to remind me of my own
    dear friends,
(For I believe lately I have thought of little
    else than of them)
Yet it remains to me a curious token, it
    makes me think of manly love;
For all that, and though the live-oak
    glistens there in Louisiana solitary in
    a wide flat space,
Uttering joyous leaves all its life without a
    friend or a lover near,
I know very well I could not.

WALT WHITMAN

Friendship is the only cement that will hold
the world together.

WOODROW WILSON

Friendship is to have the latchkey of
another's mind.

EDGAR J. GOODSPEED

A man must eat a peck of salt with his friend
before he knows him.

MIGUEL DE CERVANTES

Friends — those relations that one makes for oneself.

EUSTACHE LESCHAMPS

---

Friendship is Love without his wings.

GEORGE GORDON, LORD BYRON

---

Now, nothing makes so much impression on the heart of man as the voice of friendship when it is really known to be such; for we are aware that it never speaks to us except for our advantage. We can suppose that a friend is deceived, but not that he wishes to deceive us. Sometimes we run counter to his advice, but we never despise it.

JEAN JACQUES ROUSSEAU

---

Human friendships usually take their rise in some external detail. We catch a phrase, we hear an inflection of a voice, we notice the look of the eyes, or a movement in walking; and the tiny experience seems to us like an initiation into a new world.

ROBERT HUGH BENSON

True friendship is like sound health — the
value of it is seldom known until it be lost.

CHARLES CALEB COLTON

THE EAVESDROPPER
I keep
A steep
And precipice repose
To hear
By ear
Who are my friends and foes.

Who cries
Me wise,
He wears but friendship's guise;
Who rends me
Mends me
And he alone befriends me.

FREDERICK DRIMMER

Music I heard with you was more than
    music,
And bread I broke with you was more
    than bread.

CONRAD AIKEN

How many lack friendship rather than friends!

SENECA

---

## THE HUMAN TOUCH
'Tis the human touch in this world that
    counts,
  The touch of your hand and mine,
Which means far more to the fainting
    heart
  Than shelter and bread and wine;
For shelter is gone when the night is o'er,
  And bread lasts only a day,
But the touch of the hand and the sound
    of the voice
  Sing on in the heart alway.

SPENCER MICHAEL FREE

---

My friend is not perfect — no more am I —
And so we suit each other admirably.

ALEXANDER POPE

We cannot tell the precise moment when friendship is formed. As in filling a vessel drop by drop, there is at last a drop which makes it run over; so in a series of kindnesses there is at last one which makes the heart run over.

SAMUEL JOHNSON

Much of our dissension is due to misunderstanding, which could be put right by a few honest words and a little honest dealing. Human beings so often live at cross-purposes with each other, when a frank word, or a simple confession of wrong, almost a look or a gesture, would heal this division.

HUGH BLACK

Every man should have a fair-sized cemetery in which to bury the faults of his friends.

HENRY WARD BEECHER

To hear complaints with patience, even when complaints are vain, is one of the duties of friendship.

SAMUEL JOHNSON

## TO YOU

Stranger, if you passing meet me and desire
   to speak to me,
  why should you not speak to me?
And why should I not speak to you?

WALT WHITMAN

---

A friend should bear his friend's infirmities.

WILLIAM SHAKESPEARE

A sweet word multiplieth friends, and
appeaseth enemies, and a gracious tongue
in a good man aboundeth.

If thou wouldst get a friend, try him before
thou takest him, and do not credit him
easily.

For there is a friend for his own occasion,
and he will not abide in the day of thy
trouble.

And there is a friend that turneth to
enmity; and there is a friend that will
disclose hatred and strife and reproaches.

And there is a friend a companion at the
table, and he will not abide in the day of
distress.

A friend shall not be known in prosperity,

and an enemy shall not be hidden in adversity.

He that flingeth a stone at birds, shall drive them away: so that he that upbraideth his friend, breaketh friendship. Although thou hast drawn a sword at a friend, despair not: for there may be a returning. To a friend, if thou hast opened a sad mouth, fear not, for there may be a reconciliation: except upbraiding, and reproach, and pride, and disclosing of secrets, or a treacherous wound: for in all these cases a friend will flee away.

ECCLESIASTICUS 6:5-12, 22:19-22

However well proved a friendship may appear, there are confidences which it should not hear, and sacrifices which should not be required of it.

JOSEPH ROUX

A friend that you have to buy won't be worth what you pay for him, no matter what that may be.

GEORGE D. PRENTICE

Friendship is to be purchased only by friendship. A man may have authority over others, but he can never have their hearts but by giving his own.

THOMAS WILSON

I composed a letter to you in my mind, whilst lying awake, dwelling in a feeling manner on the fact that human beings are born into this little span of life of which the best thing is its friendships and intimacies, and soon their places will know them no more, and yet they leave their friendships and intimacies with no cultivation, to grow as they will by the roadside, expecting them to "keep" by force of mere inertia; they contribute nothing empirical to the relation, treating it as something transcendental and metaphysical altogether; whereas in truth it deserves from hour to hour the most active care and nurture and devotion.

WILLIAM JAMES

To find a friend one must close one eye — to keep him, two.

NORMAN DOUGLAS

Was it a friend or foe that spread these lies?
Nay, who but infants question in such wise,
'Twas one of my most intimate enemies.

DANTE GABRIEL ROSSETTI

## ART THOU LONELY?
Art thou lonely, O my brother?
Share thy little with another!
Stretch a hand to one unfriended,
And thy loneliness is ended.

JOHN OXENHAM

## TO FIND A FRIEND
The city's ways are not my ways, and never
   Shall I to its demands be reconciled;
I walk amid its roar and rumble, dreaming,
A cool and careful man in outward seeming,
   But in my heart a lost and lonely child.

I wear a mask, as you do and as all do,
   To hide what none has time to com-
      prehend;
A mask of settled purpose and of daring,
To hide how very little I am caring
   For anything but just to find a friend.

FRANK PUTNAM

The supreme happiness of life is the conviction of being loved for yourself, or, more correctly, being loved in spite of yourself.

VICTOR HUGO

I want someone to laugh with me, someone to be grave with me, someone to please me and help my discrimination with his or her own remark, and at times, no doubt, to admire my acuteness and penetration.

ROBERT BURNS

Ah, friend, let us be true
To one another! For the world, which seems
To lie before us like a land of dreams,
So various, so beautiful, so new,
Hath really neither joy, nor love, nor light,
Nor certitude, nor peace, nor help for pain,
And we are here as on a darkling plain
Swept with confused alarms of struggle and
     flight,
Where ignorant armies clash by night.

MATTHEW ARNOLD

What is thine is mine, and all mine is thine.

PLAUTUS

From quiet homes and first beginning,
  Out to the undiscovered ends,
There's nothing worth the wear of winning
  But laughter and the love of friends.

HILAIRE BELLOC

And Heaven protect us also from the easily offended friend who, refusing to understand once and for all that we are fond of him but that life is short and difficult and human beings capricious, watches us unceasingly so that he may interpret every manifestation of impatience or bad humor as an omen. An easily offended person will never make real friends. True friendship implies full confidence, which may only be completely given or completely withdrawn. If friendship has continually to be analyzed, nursed, and cured, it will cause more anguish than love itself, without having love's strength and its remedies.

ANDRÉ MAUROIS

Friendship based solely upon gratitude is like a photograph; with time it fades.

CARMEN SYLVA

There is an electricity about a friendship relationship. We are both more relaxed and more sensitive, more creative and more reflective, more energetic and more casual, more excited and more serene. It is as though when we come in contact with our friend we enter into a different environment.

ANDREW M. GREELEY

I sent out invitations
to summer guests.
I collected together
All my friends.
Loud talk
And simple feasting:
Discussion of philosophy,
Investigation of subtleties.
Tongues loosened
And minds at one.
Hearts refreshed
By discharge of emotion!

CH'ENG-KUNG SUI
*Translated by Arthur Waley*

Life is partly what we make it, and partly what it is made by the friends we choose.

TEHYI HSIEH

Old friends are the great blessings of one's later years. Half a word conveys one's meaning. They have a memory of the same events, have the same mode of thinking. I have young relations that may grow upon me, for my nature is affectionate, but can they grow [to be] *old* friends?

HORACE WALPOLE

Friendship always benefits; love sometimes injures.

SENECA

"Stay" is a charming word in a friend's vocabulary.

AMOS BRONSON ALCOTT

Two friendships in two breasts requires
The same aversions and desires.

JONATHAN SWIFT

If I mayn't tell you what I feel, what is the use of a friend?

WILLIAM MAKEPEACE THACKERAY

Friendships begin with liking or gratitude —
roots that can be pulled up.

GEORGE ELIOT

---

Who seeks a faultless friend remains friend-
less.

TURKISH PROVERB

## IF I CAN STOP ONE HEART FROM BREAKING

If I can stop one heart from breaking,
   I shall not live in vain;
If I can ease one life the aching,
   Or cool one pain,
Or help one lonely person
   Into happiness again
I shall not live in vain.

EMILY DICKINSON

---

No receipt [remedy] openeth the heart but a
true friend, to whom you may impart griefs,
joys, fears, hopes, suspicions, counsels, and
whatsoever lieth upon the heart to oppress
it, in a kind of civil shrift or confession.

FRANCIS BACON

Our friends interpret the world and ourselves to us, if we take them tenderly and truly.

AMOS BRONSON ALCOTT

A good motto is: Use friendliness but do not use your friends.

FRANK CRANE

Man strives for glory, honor, fame,
That all the world may know his name.
Amasses wealth by brain and hand;
Becomes a power in the land,
But when he nears the end of life
And looks back over the years of strife,
He finds that happiness depends
On none of these but love of friends.

UNKNOWN

But whoso hath this world's good, and seeth his brother have need, and shutteth up his bowels of compassion from him, how dwelleth the love of God in him?

My little children, let us not love in word, neither in tongue; but in deed and in truth.

I JOHN 3:17,18

Friendships begun in this world will be taken up again, never to be broken off.

ST. FRANCIS DE SALES

---

That friendship only is indeed genuine when two friends, without speaking a word to each other, can nevertheless find happiness in being together.

GEORG EBERS

---

I want my friend to miss me as long as I miss him.

ST. AUGUSTINE

---

Friendship makes prosperity brighter, while it lightens adversity by sharing its griefs and anxieties.

CICERO

It may be a cold, clammy thing to say, but those that treat friendship the same as any other selfishness seem to get the most out of it.

E.W. HOWE

Training and tradition may have cast us in dissimilar molds, but the basic stuff of our humanity is pathetically the same. It is this realization that now makes every stranger accessible to me. He may be a barber or a banknote engraver, but it is almost certain that he can tell me something that will heighten my mental stature or increase my spiritual gauge . . . By far the larger part of our human race is composed of interesting and friendly members, all eager to know each other. And I have yet to see the person who did not become more attractive and more alive for laying aside his too-prized reserve and mingling on equal terms with other members of our common, struggling, hungering human family.

HENRY MORTON ROBINSON

To our friends, who know the worst about us but refuse to believe it.

OLD TOAST

If you want to make a dangerous man your friend, let him do you a favor.

LEWIS E. LAWES

The time to make friends is before you need them.

PROVERB

All that this world knows of living
Lies in giving — and more giving;
He that keeps, be sure he loses —
Friendship grows by what it uses.

ALEXANDER MACLEAN

We talk of choosing our friends, but friends are self-elected.

RALPH WALDO EMERSON

GOD MAKE ME WORTHY OF MY FRIENDS

It is my joy to find
   At every turning of the road
The strong arm of a comrade kind
   To help me onward with my load;
And since I have no gold to give
   'Tis love alone must make amends,
My only prayer is while I live —
   God make me worthy of my friends.

UNKNOWN

Love Him, and keep Him for thy Friend,
who, when all go away, will not forsake thee,
nor suffer thee to perish at the last.

THOMAS À KEMPIS

---

### I SOUGHT MY SOUL

I sought my soul,
  But my soul I could not see.
I sought my God,
  But my God eluded me.
I sought my brother
  And I found all three.

UNKNOWN

---

Real friends are those who, when you've
made a fool of yourself, don't feel that you've
done a permanent job.

ERWIN T. RANDALL

---

Elizabeth Barrett Browning asked Charles
Kingsley, "What is the secret of your life?
Tell me that I may make mine beautiful,
too." He replied: "I had a friend."

# ACKNOWLEDGEMENTS

The editor and the publisher have made every effort to trace the ownership of all copyrighted material and to secure permission from copyright holders of such material. In the event of any question arising as to the use of any material the publisher and editor, while expressing regret for inadvertent error, will be pleased to make the necessary corrections in future printings. Thanks are due to the following authors, publishers, publications and agents for permission to use the material indicated.

ALFRED A. KNOPF, INC., for "Inviting Guests" by Ch'eng-kung Sui from *A Hundred and Seventy Chinese Poems* translated by Arthur Waley, copyright 1919 and renewed 1947 by Arthur Waley.

HARPER'S MAGAZINE, for "The Wall" by Elizabeth Morrow, copyright 1926 by Harper's Magazine, reprinted in the May 1926 issue.